Critical
Thinking

The *Student Essentials* series

STUDENT
ESSENTIALS

Critical
Thinking

Debra Hills

trotman t

Student Essentials: Critical Thinking

This first edition published in 2011 by Trotman Publishing, a division of Crimson Publishing Ltd., Westminster House, Kew Road, Richmond, Surrey TW9 2ND

© Trotman Publishing 2011

Author Debra Hills

Designed by Andy Prior

British Library Cataloguing in Publication Data
A catalogue record for this book is available from the British Library

ISBN 978 1 84455 274 0

Typeset by IDSUK (DataConnection) Ltd

Printed and bound in the UK by Ashford Colour Press Gosport, Hants

Contents

Introduction

A common complaint among university tutors is that students do not think critically enough. Essays are 'too descriptive', 'have no evidence' or 'show no argument'. However, while students are expected to think critically and assessments are graded on this ability, a critical approach is rarely actually explained.

What is critical thinking?

In everyday English, being critical means finding fault:

  " *The tutor criticised me for jumping to conclusions.* "

Another common meaning of critical is 'highly important':

  " *Managing your time is critical if you want to do well at university.* "

Critical also describes the work of those who review films, books and music. Film critics, for instance, don't just say whether or not they enjoyed a film; they judge the film's strengths and weaknesses using criteria such as the script, the acting and the direction.

This third meaning is closest to what is meant by 'critical' in academic studies.

A critical approach applies to all aspects of university study: not only reading and writing assignments but listening in lectures, giving presentations and speaking in seminars. It involves a number of skills:

- precision both in understanding academic texts and in writing your own
- being able to form and to follow arguments
- logical reasoned thinking
- knowing when to take information at face value and when to challenge
- analysing and evaluating information
- selecting the right knowledge for the task
- understanding issues from perspectives other than your own.

Clearly, the 'thinking' is as crucial as the 'critical'. Sounds like hard work! So why bother?

The need to think critically

You need to think critically because your tutors expect it. Every assessment, from coursework to exams, is marked according to an agreed set of standards: the **assessment criteria**. Each course has its own criteria but certain requirements for a top grade appear across the board. Here are some of the more common ones.

- Demonstrates an ability to think critically (covered in Chapters 1 and 2)
- Good depth of analysis (covered in Chapters 4 and 8)
- Identifies key debates (covered in Chapters 3, 6 and 7)
- Strong argument (covered in Chapters 3, 4, 5 and 8)
- Evidence of independent thinking (covered in Chapters 2 and 7)
- Extensive range of sources, applied with insight (covered in Chapter 6)

■ Good evaluation of source material (covered in Chapters 4 and 5).

All of these require critical thinking and are dealt with in this book. Now look at some of the criteria used to award lower scores:

■ overly descriptive
■ no argument
■ inappropriate/irrelevant material
■ limited reasoning
■ opinions expressed without evidence
■ weakly structured argument.

These comments are linked to a lack of critical thinking; their exact meanings will become more apparent as you read on.

Whatever your subject area or discipline, you will be expected to think critically. This book aims to get you started, explaining how to apply critical thinking to your reading and written assignments. While there's no short cut to thinking critically, the more you apply your critical skills, the deeper you will engage with your subject until it becomes a natural way to approach your studies. Oh yes, and get those top grades!

PART 1

Developing a critical state of mind

It's all very well being told to think critically, but what exactly does this mean? Part 1 spells out what a critical approach entails, beginning with why it is necessary and exploring common barriers to effective critical thinking. Chapter 2 outlines the six steps to critical understanding, while Chapter 3 analyses argument – the heart of critical thinking.

1 Preparing to think critically

To understand why critical thinking is so crucial, we need to differentiate between the types of knowledge used at university level. Then we can look at how our **own** thinking patterns, such as jumping to conclusions or insisting we know best, can often obstruct effective thought.

Approaches to teaching and learning at university

It may come as a surprise to learn that at university, there is no-one to **teach** you! The role of a university tutor is:

- to **guide** you in your studies by designing a stimulating syllabus and providing you with a reading list
- to **assist** you with your learning through lectures and seminars.

Tutors might point out misinterpretations of ideas or explain complex notion but they will not tell you what to think. To put it plainly, they are not teachers.

Another, often welcome, surprise is the lighter timetable. Many first-year students are delighted to find whole days lecture- and seminar-free. Don't sign up for the synchronised swimming team just yet, however! You need this time to tackle your reading list and complete your written assignments.

At university, the word 'homework' is replaced by the phrase 'independent study'. And the key to independent study? Critical thinking, of course! Critical thinking is necessary because knowledge at undergraduate level is no longer straightforward. Gone are the days of the 'learn and churn' approach of reproducing facts; at university, knowledge becomes more complex. Broadly speaking, subject knowledge can be classified into two types: uncontested and contested.

Different types of knowledge

Uncontested knowledge

This includes much of what you learned at school; for example, the reproduction patterns of the amoeba or the date of the Battle of Hastings. Facts, laws, principles – anything which can be checked and proven – are uncontested; taken as true unless proven otherwise. As an undergraduate, you need to become familiar with the specialist uncontested knowledge in your discipline. However, this knowledge will only form part of the picture. You will need to be just as familiar with the contested knowledge of your subject.

Contested knowledge

'Contested' means open to question. Theories, ideas, and perspectives can be challenged, questioned and disputed. Psychology students, for instance, ask whether or not human intelligence is genetic or due to environmental factors; astronomers attempt to find out the exact age of the planet Earth. For questions like these, there is not one answer but a number of competing perspectives which may contradict and even undermine each other. Moreover, what seems certain at a basic level is often questioned at higher levels. A once simple word like 'freedom', for example, can be the subject of an entire dissertation.

While uncontested knowledge is assumed to be true and can be applied to problems without question, contested knowledge needs to be examined critically. With this type of knowledge, the lack of a single, correct answer may initially be frustrating. However, when dealing with a contested issue, the aim is not to give **the** answer; the aim is to show, after a full consideration of all sides of the issue, what the writer believes to be the most **convincing** answer.

With such a large amount of contested knowledge at university, it is crucial to take a critical approach. But there's one last potential obstacle to critical thinking you need to face: yourself.

Getting to know yourself – critically

Here's a short thinking exercise which will help you spot any short-circuits in your own ability to think critically. Look at the statement below and decide whether you agree or disagree. How strongly do you feel about it? What are the reasons for your answer?

> " *Using Facebook extensively can diminish a person's intellectual ability.* "

Now, decide which of the responses below best suits your own.

1. Why argue with something as ridiculous as this?

2. It's definitely true/definitely false.

3. It's true! A friend of mine spent all day on Facebook and ended up dropping out of college.

9

4. Who cares?

5. I don't know.

6. I'd say it's 50% true and 50% false.

7. I agree/disagree for a number of reasons but I'd need more information before I gave a definitive answer.

Comments on responses

1. Be careful. Dismissing everything is as closed-minded as believing everything. Critical thinking needs an open mind. Assuming you are right without considering other perspectives shows no deep thought.

2. Is anything really so black and white? Total conviction of your own viewpoint suggests inflexible thinking with counterarguments ignored and debates simplified.

3. Personal anecdotes hold no sway in academic thinking. You're right to justify your position with an example but only those from academic texts or studies can be used to support a viewpoint.

4. Shrugging your shoulders indicates no thinking at all.

5. and **6.** Sitting on the fence may feel safe; perhaps you worry your answer is 'wrong' or that your opinion isn't important. However, opting out of a debate suggests a lack of engagement and is likely to lead to average marks.

7. Yes! We have a burgeoning critical thinker in our midst.

All of these responses are common. It's normal to dismiss an argument because we don't like it. Lots of people thrive on proving the other person wrong. But these stances fail to show consideration of all sides of the issue. Equally, it is common to feel we don't know enough about an issue to take any stance. However, not knowing enough is an invitation to think critically: to read different perspectives and decide which are most closely aligned to our own.

Most of us fall into one of two categories: over-opinionated (like responses 1 to 3) and under-opinionated (like responses 4 to 6). Moreover, we may be over-opinionated in certain circumstances and under-opinionated in others. Both create barriers to critical thinking. However, each can be rectified by a degree of self-awareness.

Over-opinionated

In family arguments, winners aren't necessarily those with the best reasoning skills or most knowledge of the issue. Winners are often the loudest shouters, the ones who won't back down and refuse to see things from any perspective other than their own. These tactics won't work at university. This is because the purpose of argument at university isn't to win; it is to gain a deeper understanding of an issue.

It is human nature to judge. However, critical thinking is about standing back from instant judgements until you know more. It is about being open-minded enough to allow new information to change your ideas or perspective. Education can shake your belief system. But only if you let it.

Under-opinionated

Perhaps you read a text and agree with the writer. Then you read one which contradicts the first. This is also convincing. You're worried that the more you read, the less you know what to think. Taking the middle way is the safest option.

Not necessarily. If Smith argues that British school children should be given machine guns as protection from bullies and Davis strongly disagrees, would you decide that half the children in the UK should be armed as a compromise? Sometimes an extreme view **is** the most defensible.

Similarly, concluding an essay with *'there are both advantages and disadvantages'* is circular – we all know **that**; it's why you were set the question! The reader wants to know, now that you have read and considered all arguments, what is the **best** stance to take and why? Chapter 3, on argument, will help you to build an informed stance.

Other barriers to critical thinking

1. Getting upset or annoyed if someone disagrees with you.

2. Unchallenged thinking. You, your parents and your friends think the same so you **must** be right.

3. A competitive nature: determination to win every argument – whatever it takes!

4. Refusing to listen to arguments you don't like.

5. Making instant judgements and sticking to them. This misses the point of education – to explore issues and fully consider implications.

These barriers tend to be fairly entrenched and we can't expect to overcome them overnight. But being self-aware and spotting our own tendencies towards certain thought patterns is a real start. Do you recognise yourself in any of the barriers above? Be on guard for barriers such as these, ready to combat them if you notice yourself reacting in your usual way.

There's one final barrier to critical thinking which needs to be examined; one which is so commonplace, it deserves a section of its own: habits of thought.

Habits of thought

Have you ever been surprised by a twist at the end of a film? The hero's best friend was the murderous blackmailer? If a film is convincing, we tend to miss the clues that all is not as it seems and watch with our usual habits of thought; e.g. best friends can be trusted.

With a habit of thought, the brain stops trying to assess, categorise or understand, economising effort and saving thought processes for when needed. Our day-to-day lives rely on them: we get up, shower and have breakfast without agonising over whether someone has planted a bomb in the bathroom or poisoned our cornflakes. Academic study, however, needs these thought processes! Habits of thought have to be challenged if we want to think critically.

Let's take an example. A report of a clinical trial shows that children taking fish-oil supplements performed better in their GCSE exams than those who did not. Goodness, what a result! You're not surprised; you already knew that fish-oil was good for the brain. This trial proves it.

Stop! You are acting on habits of thought!

Look a little closer. The study was funded by Cod-Eye, a major fish-oil manufacturer. Oh dear, there may be some vested interests. You look closer still. How **much** better were the GCSE results? On average, pupils gained one grade higher in one subject. So not much. And the experiment has not been repeated so results cannot be verified. Not such a conclusive result, after all.

We tend to believe evidence for what we think we already know; it's the simplest option. Academia, however, expects complexity and tutors are quick to spot habits of thinking. We need to check instant judgements through careful, critical reasoning.

So now we are on guard for barriers to critical thinking; it's time to find out how we **should** think.

How to think

No-one can tell you how to think! At university, you have to show you can think for yourself. However, Socrates, writing 2,500 years ago, is a good place to start:

❝ *True knowledge exists in knowing that you know nothing.* ❞

Accepting that you do not have all the answers can be extremely liberating and leads to a genuinely open mind. Stephen Fry on *QI* delights in learning that the Earth has seven moons or that Queen Victoria smoked cannabis. Having the flexibility to modify your views as you learn more will give you a stronger foundation for further learning and understanding.

If you still want an answer on how to think, then read on. Chapter 2 examines how different assignments require you to think in different ways.

Tips for top scores

■ Think about a key debate in your subject. Where do you stand? Why? What other perspectives can you think of on this issue? Which one do you most disagree with? Try to see the issue from this perspective. Understanding alternative viewpoints will make your thinking stronger.

■ Look at an assignment or seminar title and decide your basic stance **before** opening a book. Notice how the reading affects your stance – either strengthening or weakening it. After reading each text, note down any changes in your perspective. If there are none, be wary – is there any reason your viewpoint is so entrenched?

✓ Dos	✗ Don'ts
✓ Assume your thinking is imprecise, inaccurate and illogical. Subjecting yourself to scrutiny should keep you sharp.	✗ Assume that 'criticise' is negative; it's about pointing out strengths as much as weaknesses.
✓ Know your weaknesses and work on them, whether it is a tendency to jump to conclusions or to sit on the fence.	✗ Waste time questioning uncontested knowledge, e.g. 'is over 70% of the Earth's surface really covered by oceans'?
✓ Take a stance of some sort. Even if you only agree 51%, you've shown you have weighed up the evidence and used it to come to a conclusion.	✗ Get upset or annoyed if an opinion is different from yours. Work on distancing yourself from these emotions.

2 Taking a critical approach

Your mind is open; you are on guard for habits of thought. You're aware of the key debates in your subject and know that much of what you read is likely to be contradicted and challenged, especially in disciplines dealing with human behaviour or where interpretation plays a key role. Time to find out what's involved in a critical approach.

Let's go back to the most common complaint made by tutors about student writing: it is too descriptive.

Descriptive writing and critical writing

Look at the box below and notice the differences between descriptive writing and critical writing.

Descriptive writing	Critical writing
states what a theory or idea is	evaluates this theory or idea by examining its argument
describes a process; shows how something works	shows the strengths and weaknesses of this process or suggests a better alternative
lists ideas, details and information	relates these ideas to the question under study; evaluates the importance of each and shows links, parallels and contrasts in the information
states what other writers have said	makes a convincing argument in answer to a specific question

Description has its place in academic writing but it is only **one step** in a critical approach. So, how do you move from descriptive writing to critical writing and gain those top grades? Ironically, to give effective answers, you need to ask the right questions. This means moving beyond the **what, where** and **who** (descriptive questions) to the **why, what if** and beyond (critical questions). Tutors set particular questions for a reason; these questions provide clues as to what you're supposed to *do* with the knowledge you encounter. Let's see these clues in action.

Steps involved in critical thinking

The steps involved in critical thinking start simply and become increasingly demanding. Each step is a necessary part of the thinking process: if you haven't done the reading or attended lectures then you won't **know** (step 1) and won't be able to move further forward. **Evaluation** (step 6) assumes steps 1 to 5 as part of its skills set. You need to learn to work through each step to be able to truly grasp critical thinking.

QUICK TIP

For each step, there are example questions taken from undergraduate exam papers. Think about questions in your own subject area and which steps they are asking you to take.

Knowledge and comprehension

Step 1: Knowledge
This is the first stage when you come across something new. Your knowledge is shown by the ability to recall, repeat, memorise and reproduce. Questions such as the ones below often form part of a longer question where the aim is to ensure accurate basic knowledge:

❝ Name *the three most commonly used metal alloys for implantation. (Materials)* **❞**

❝ Define *neoplasia. (Medicine)* **❞**

But being able to quote a Shakespearian sonnet or list the elements of the periodic table does not necessarily mean that you understand. This is covered in the next step.

Step 2: Comprehension
Until you understand something, you cannot work with it critically. In your writing, the ability to effectively paraphrase (put a writer's ideas into your own words) shows that you actually comprehend what you have read. You'll need to do this when referring to theories or ideas. Again, questions of a technical or theoretical nature often begin by testing comprehension:

❝ Explain *'the Bruun rule'. (Geography)* **❞**

❝ *Using domestic hot water as an example,* **describe** *the operating systems of a solar thermal system. (Engineering)* **❞**

So far, so straightforward. 'Know and show' are the foundations of critical thinking. However, they are **only** the foundations. At university, you need to **use** your new knowledge.

> **QUICK TIP**
> When using ideas from texts, you must put them into your words, not only to show comprehension but to avoid accusations of plagiarism.

Application and analysis

Step 3: Application
Here, you show you can **apply** theories and arguments. In vocational subjects such as nursing, as well as in science

19

subjects, the ability to put theory into practice is crucial. Case studies, experiments and problem solving are common coursework assignments which ask you to use your theoretical knowledge for a practical purpose:

> **"** *Write a patient* **case study** *focusing on the multi-disciplinary approaches to health provision. (Nursing)* **"**

> **"** *Use the Bruun rule to explain the erosion of sandy shores in the Farne Islands. (Geology)* **"**

In science and vocational subjects, a substantial part of your study involves applying theories and principles and analysing the results. In arts and social sciences, however, application comes after analysis and evaluation – you only apply a theory or idea once it has been critically assessed.

Applying knowledge shows it has a real purpose. However, applying it without question means accepting it at face value. That's fine with uncontested knowledge such as accepted facts and widely used principles. However, contested knowledge should never be accepted at face value; it needs to be analysed carefully.

Step 4: Analysis
This is where the thinking cap comes on. Analysis involves digging deep. It means examining ideas carefully, breaking them down and questioning then closely. Seeing patterns in data, understanding how parts of a system are organised, and reading between the lines are all part of analysis. As you can imagine, this is a crucial part of critical thinking. Questions which ask you to

compare and contrast, to explain **why** or to examine an argument are asking for analysis:

> " **Explain the differences and similarities** *between the following types of market: Perfect Competition, Monopolistic Competition and Monopoly. (Business Studies)* "

> " **Examine the role** *'androgyny' plays in the arguments from Elaine Showalter's A Literature of Their Own. (English)* "

Analysis, therefore, involves close reading of one particular text or argument (see Chapters 4 and 5). However, at university, you're expected to read **lots** of texts. You need to analyse **all** of the main theoretical positions and central arguments in your field. This leads us to the final two steps.

Synthesis and evaluation

Step 5: Synthesis
Synthesis means bringing together everything you've read: selecting relevant information; noting recurrent themes and showing how ideas from different sources link (see Chapter 6). The more you read, the wider a pool of knowledge you will be able to draw from. It is not only theoretical assignments which expect a high level of synthesis. Questions asking for a creative response expect your answer to be based on the ideas you have analysed and found strongest, most relevant and most useful. For example:

> " **Develop** *a short take-off and landing air ambulance. (Aerospace Engineering)* "

❝ Do the techniques *for the interpretation of dreams described by Freud in* **On Dreams** *help us with the interpretation of other kinds of writing? (English)* ❞

Questions like the ones above also expect an element of evaluation. Indeed, once you synthesise, it is difficult **not** to evaluate; that is, to make a judgement on what you have read.

Step 6: Evaluation
This is the highest level of critical thinking. Evaluation asks: what do you make of the competing arguments and contradictory theories? This is not a snap decision! To evaluate, you have to know and understand (steps 1 and 2); analyse texts carefully (step 4); see them in relation to the others you have read (step 5) and relate them to your question (step 3). Questions asking for an evaluative, and therefore rigorously critical, approach are extremely common in both undergraduate exams and coursework assignments:

❝ Do you find *liberal theories of international trade convincing? (Economics)* ❞

❝ To what extent *does the US Constitution protect interpersonal relationships? (Law)* ❞

When answering this type of question, you need to go further than reporting what others have said; you need to **draw conclusions**. Yes, some background information and theoretical underpinning will be necessary to support your case (description, steps 1 and 2), but your job is to **use** what you have read in order to build your own individual argument. The chapters in Parts 2 and 3 of this book should help you with evaluation.

Adapting an analytical and evaluative approach to your studies brings a bonus: it makes you more active and engaged in your learning. But there is something specific you should be analysing and evaluating: argument. Arguments form the backbone of the texts that you read and the assignments you write. The next chapter looks at argument in a university context.

University teaching operates from the deep-rooted belief that knowledge grows from debate and that questioning brings a deeper understanding: the Socratic method of learning. However, question words such as **describe** or **discuss** may mean different things in different disciplines. See Chapter 9 for more on the differences in critical thinking in different disciplines.

Tips for top scores

■ If you haven't already, read an introduction/overview to your subject. You need to identify the fundamental concepts and debates in your subject as soon as you can. You cannot think deeply without knowing the basics.

■ Look at past exam papers on your library website to see the kind of questions that are typical in your discipline.

■ Be on guard for seemingly simple questions, such as *'What is democracy?'* These **demand** evaluation.

✓ Dos	✗ Don'ts
✓ Read as widely as you can, especially for coursework assignments.	✗ Describe in too much detail unless specifically asked. You need to carefully select what needs to be explained or described before moving onto analysis.
✓ Look at assignment questions carefully to work out what type of thinking is required.	✗ Forget that in order to evaluate well, you'll need to be able to understand, apply, analyse and synthesise – there's no short cut!
✓ Think about the texts you read. Are they applying? Analysing? Evaluating?	✗ Memorise without understanding – you'll never get any further than step 1.

3 Argument

Once you can argue well, particularly in writing, you have mastered the core attribute for university education. However, lack of argument in student writing is a frequent grumble of tutors. Look back at the assessment criteria in the Introduction and you'll see that high scores are given for:

- identifies key debates
- strong argument.

Papers with a weakly structured argument, or no argument at all, unsurprisingly, score lowly. This chapter sets out exactly what an argument is. By working through it, you'll be better able to find key ideas in readings and lectures, participate effectively in seminar discussions and, of course, write critically.

What an argument is: premises and claims

An academic argument needs certain components in order to be effective. Look below:

   " *Memory isn't that important for academic success.* **"**

This is not an argument it is an opinion. It makes a claim but gives no reasons (or premises). Feedback from tutors such as 'where is your evidence?' means you have made claims without any premises. As such, you haven't made an argument. Look at the next example:

> " Much undergraduate assessment is coursework. Moreover, in some exams students are able to take in reference books. Thus, memory isn't that important for academic success. "

Now we've got an argument! Here the writer gives premises which attempt to **persuade** the reader that the final sentence, the claim, should be accepted. An argument makes a claim based on premises with the aim of persuading the reader of its truth.

Premise(s) + a claim + an attempt to persuade = an argument

Look again at the second example. The first two sentences are **premises** which lead to the third sentence. This third sentence is the point the writer is making: **the claim**. The claim can come at the end, as it did in the example; at the beginning to draw attention to the point being made, or even in the middle. But it has to come! Tutor comments such as *'Where's your argument?'* indicate that the essay may have put forward relevant information, but it hasn't shown **why** this is relevant; it hasn't drawn any conclusions. Let's look more closely at the components of an argument: premises and claim.

Key components of an argument

Premises

There's a slight, but important, difference between a reason and a premise.

- Reason: a fact, condition or situation which leads to a claim. (i.e. based on uncontested knowledge) *Sam and Pam share identical DNA. They must be twins.*
- Premise: a principle or statement which you **believe to be true** which leads to a claim. (i.e. based on either contested or uncontested knowledge). *Sam and Pam share a bedsit. It must be cramped.*

Since you might believe something to be true because it is true, premise covers both terms.

In your writing assessments, any claims you make need to be supported by academically sound premises. These include:

- arguments from key thinkers in your field (authors on your reading list)
- evidence from research data (statistical, scientific, historical)
- commonly accepted ideas, theories and principles, specific to your subject.

Don't forget that the premises are the reasons you are making your claim. The more persuasive they are, the more convincing your claim is likely to be.

Claims

A claim is just that: not necessarily **the** answer but what the writer argues (**claims**) is the **best** answer, based on the premises they have given. The claim is the nucleus of the argument. It answers **why; why** the writer quoted Weber; **why** they provided a particular graph. A claim indicates the writer's stance, or voice. No claim = no voice.

In arts, humanities and social sciences, claims are more likely to deal with human reasoning rather than verifiable facts. For instance:

> **"** If Nelson had not prevailed at Trafalgar, the British Empire could not have happened. **"**

We cannot know this for sure. This claim is bound to be contested. However, with convincing premises, a strong argument can be built.

The claims are the core of the writer's arguments. Read without looking out for claims and you're likely to miss the point. You can find the main claims:

- in the abstract of a journal, in the introduction and at the end of the paper under 'conclusion'
- in the initial and final paragraphs of a chapter
- towards the end of the first paragraph of an essay *(this essay will)* and in the final paragraph.

Claims should be easy to find. Academic writers do not hide their argument but state it explicitly. Yours must be equally explicit in your own writing.

So, now we've got the idea of what an argument is, we need to be clear about what an argument isn't.

What an argument isn't

Essay feedback such as *'doesn't address the question'* or *'not relevant'* suggests the writer has taken background information and presented it as central, thereby side-lining the key arguments. This is understandable; arguments are often embedded in description, explanation and examples and it can be hard to pinpoint the claims. Some key sentence types **look** like arguments but remember, an argument has three essential ingredients: premises, a claim and an attempt to persuade.

The following sentence types give a fuller picture to the overall argument but you need to be clear: they are **not** arguments. Let's see why.

Descriptions

Descriptions are written to inform, not to persuade. For example, in an essay on the electoral system of the UK, you may need to describe how it works (the first two steps of a critical approach) before you critique it:

> **"** *Parliamentary elections in the UK are held using the single member plurality system, commonly known as the 'first past the post system'. This is where the highest polling candidate of every constituency wins a seat in government.* **"**

This informs the reader but does not present an argument.

Explanations

Because an explanation often has reasons linked to a conclusion, it can get confused with argument. Again, however, an explanation is not trying to persuade but to inform. It shows comprehension: step 2 of a critical approach. With an explanation, the writer assumes a statement **is** true and works to explain **why** this is so.

> **"** *In the UK, no politician can stay in power indefinitely. This is because elections are held roughly every five years.* **"**

In this example, the second sentence is not justifying the first; it simply explains. If an explanation **is** used to justify the writer's conclusion, then it becomes a premise and part of the argument. Look below. The second sentence both explains the first and leads to the claim of the final sentence:

> **"** *Parliamentary elections in the UK are held using the single member plurality system, commonly known as the 'first past the post system'. This is where the highest polling candidate of every constituency wins a seat in government. Clearly, such a system is unfair for those parties consistently coming second in every seat.* **"**

Otherwise you're in danger of a *'so what?'* comment from your tutor. When writing an explanation, make sure you know **why** you are writing it and how it relates to the main claim.

Summaries

A summary repeats the key points made without including new material or making a claim (again showing comprehension, step 2 of the critical approach). However, since it may use a signal word like **so** or **therefore**), it can get confused with an argument. Again, the crucial difference is that the summary is not attempting to persuade:

> **"** *From an early age, school children are socialised into expectations of what is appropriate in class; how texts should be used and how they should engage in the learning process. Education, therefore, is culturally determined.* **"**

Here, **therefore** signals that the writer is summing up the previous sentence; rephrasing it in fewer words. Again, summaries are a useful part of academic writing but they are not arguments and do not indicate the writer's stance.

Reports of arguments

This is where many good students come unstuck. Using academic sources is essential for building a written argument at university. A common problem, however, is to put forward the key thinkers' arguments, but not your own. This shows you can paraphrase (step 2 yet again!) but nothing more. Look at the sentence below:

❝ *Barnes (2008) argues that free trade increases the global level of output because it permits specialisation among countries.* ❞

This tells us what Barnes thinks, but not where the writer stands in relation to it. When the author is the subject of your sentence (*Barnes argues* . . .) or if you begin the sentence with *'according to Barnes'*, you are reporting. This is fine if the sentence is a premise. In this case, make sure that a claim drawn from the premise soon follows:

❝ *Barnes (2008) argues that free trade increases the global level of output because it permits specialisation among countries. Free trade thus allows each country to work to its best capacity.* ❞

With the additional sentence, you have drawn a conclusion from the information; you have made a claim.

Of course, working out the function of a sentence is not an exact science. There'll be times when judging whether it is a description or an argument is nigh on impossible. But asking what a sentence is doing is a good general guide to finding the argument and, in your own writing, to keeping the argument on track.

Overall arguments and subsidiary arguments

An overall argument is the purpose of the whole piece. It can be book length, with premises divided into chapters. Each chapter can be seen as a subsidiary argument which **contributes** to the overall argument. In journal papers and essays, the overall argument is the aim of the piece while the subsidiary arguments are the building blocks. Subsidiary arguments work to persuade both in their own right and as part of the overall argument.

Tips for top scores

■ When reading complex arguments, look for claims. This will help you to locate the rest of the argument. Ask yourself, *what is the writer trying to persuade me of?*

■ Limit note taking to arguments; these are what you need to engage with. The rest is background; there to provide a context.

■ Keep tutor comments in mind when planning essays: *'where's your evidence'* (no premises); *'so what?'* (no claim).

■ In seminar discussions, keep your argument academic by only making claims with informed premises behind them.

✓ Dos	✗ Don'ts
✓ Ask yourself what the function of each sentence is. Is it a claim? A description? This will help you find the line of reasoning.	✗ Forget that an argumentative essay needs a stance. Don't write until you are clear what you are trying to convince your reader of.
✓ Slow down when you've found the argument in a text. This is the key part and you need to be sure you understand it.	✗ Make claims without premises when you are writing essays. Similarly, don't include information which doesn't lead to a claim. Without both premises and claims, you haven't got an argument.
✓ In essays, make sure your overall argument is stated in the introduction. This is often the final sentence and starts with *'This essay will . . .'*	✗ Forget the last key element in argument; the attempt to persuade.

PART 2

Assessing arguments

Now we're clear about what argument is, we need to be able to analyse it effectively. Part 2 is about analysis and evaluation. Chapter 4 looks at how an argument is structured and how choice of premises affects the strength of claims. Chapter 5 zooms in on the finer detail, exploring how unfounded assumptions and ineffective language weaken argument. In Chapter 6, we zoom back out, situating the argument in the bigger picture by setting it into context and comparing it to others.

4 Identifying and assessing a line of reasoning

With a claim, premises and an attempt to persuade, we've got an argument. Great! But if we simply restate key arguments, we've moved no further than showing comprehension (step 2 of a critical approach). Remember the assessment criteria from the Introduction?

- Good depth of analysis.
- Strong argument.
- Good evaluation of source material.

To analyse and evaluate the key arguments in our discipline, we need to locate and assess the line of reasoning in an argument. If it is strong, the argument holds; if there's a weakness, the argument can be challenged.

Following a line of reasoning

The line of reasoning is the way premises and claims link to create a chain of thought. A strong argument moves in a clear direction with premises supporting, justifying, and making it reasonable to believe the truth of the claim. Let's take a look at four common ways in which a line of reasoning works.

1. Sometimes one reason will be enough:

> " *Taking a part-time job while at university forces the student to manage their study time productively* **(Premise)**. *Therefore, those who work often stay on top of their studies better than those who don't* **(Claim)**. "

As a diagram this becomes:

P *(premise)* → **C** *(claim)*

2. Look at the next example:

> " *Taking a part-time job while at university forces the student to manage their study time productively* **(Premise 1)**. *Moreover, working students also learn how to interact with managers and colleagues* **(Premise 2)**. *Thus, with these skills, they may well be at an advantage when it comes to graduate recruitment* **(Claim)**. "

Here, there are two separate premises. If you take one away, the argument still stands.

P1 + P2 → **C**

There could be three or more premises all dealing with separate points and all leading to the same claim.

3. Look at the next example. How is it different from the second?

> " *Taking a part-time job while at university forces the student to manage their study time productively*

(Premise 1). *It also shows employers the student is punctual and reliable in the workplace* **(Premise 2)**. *Such attributes may therefore put the part-time worker at an advantage when it comes to graduate recruitment* **(Claim)**. "

Here the reasons act together and reinforce each other. Managing time as a student and managing time as an employee are related. As a diagram it looks like this:

P1 + P2 → C

Again, there may be two, three or more related reasons working together.

4. Look at the second sentence in the next example. What is its function – premise or claim?

" *Taking a part-time job while at university forces the student to manage their study time productively* **(Premise)**. *These skills may put the part-time worker at an advantage when it comes to graduate recruitment* **(?)**. *Employers look for graduates who can show they are independent and reliable* **(Claim)**. "

The second sentence is definitely a claim because it is a conclusion based on the premise in the first sentence. But read the second and third sentences again. Can you see how the second sentence works as a reason for the third? The second sentence has a double function: it's both a premise and a conclusion. This type of sentence is commonly called an **intermediate conclusion (IC)**.

P *(1 or more)* → **IC** *(new P)* → **C**

A chain of intermediate conclusions can be very strong but must be assessed carefully; if there is weakness in one stage the whole argument topples like a house of cards.

When constructing your own arguments, plan out the line of reasoning **before** you start writing. This will ensure you are not hopping from one idea to the next and avoid feedback such as *'confused'* or *'lack of organisation'*. It should also keep you focused on the question and make you less likely to digress.

Once you've found the argument and worked out the line of reasoning it's time for evaluation: what makes an argument strong or weak?

A strong argument

An argument is strong if:

1. each premise in the line of reasoning is judged as accurate
2. the claim drawn follows logically from the premises.

We'll assume here that the premises **are** accurate and save that assessment for Chapter 5. Here, we are concerned with 2.: Does the claim follow logically from the premises? Are the premises strong enough so that there is only one claim possible: the one which is given?

Assessing the line of reasoning can be difficult when an argument is complex; you have to **understand** it first. By separating out the premises and working out where they link, the argument will be easier to analyse and to evaluate.

QUICK TIP

We need to recognise a strong argument regardless of whether or not we disagree and recognise a weak one even when it supports our view. Pointing out weaknesses in counterarguments is important but it is just as important to acknowledge any relevant strengths.

Reconstructing the argument

This involves careful reading. An argument can consist of a short paragraph, several pages or even an entire book. To reconstruct it:

1. start with the main claim: what does the writer want to persuade readers to believe?

2. identify the premises: what are the writer's reasons for this claim?

3. identify the structure: do premises work separately or together? Do they build to an intermediate conclusion which then leads to the next claim?

Let's tidy up this paragraph. Decide the function of each sentence. Which ones form part of the argument?

> " *The purpose of a university education should not be to prepare students for the workplace but to give them space to think and allow them to explore key concepts and debates (1). Knowledge at this level is less about regurgitating facts and more about questioning, applying and using information (Brown, 1989) (2). Independent, critical thinking is a transferrable skill, invaluable in the workplace (3). A doctor decides*

whether or not to operate, a lawyer prepares a case, a TV researcher selects key information (4). In one's personal life, without the ability to think well and for oneself, one's quality of life is diminished (Burns, 2001) (5). Research suggests that a major cause of depression is the feeling of not being in control of life decisions (6). "

(1) is the claim: university education should be about learning to think.

(2) gives an explanation of the claim: knowledge should be about questioning, applying and using information.

(3) is a premise: clear thinking is an invaluable skill.

(4) illustrates (3): it is an example.

(5) is a second premise: without independent thinking the quality of life is diminished.

(6) gives an example of this.

In this argument, the premises work separately from each other.

P1 + P2 → C

Laid out like this, it is easier to see what is key (the claims and premises) and what is extraneous. Assessing now becomes more straightforward; you can pinpoint the exact premise which is weak or which gives strength to the argument. This is exactly what those tutors want; analysis and evaluation!

Assessing the line of reasoning

Relevant premises

To be relevant, the premise needs to **lead** to the conclusion. Without it, the claim is unable to stand.

Look at the two sentences below. Which has a relevant premise?

1. *Using Facebook extensively can diminish a person's intellectual ability. In 2010, 18 million people were registered users.*
2. *Using Facebook extensively can diminish a person's intellectual ability. Sachs (2008) found that the IQ of Facebook users diminishes with use.*

In 1., the premise makes no difference to the claim – it might be true but it doesn't form part of the argument. In 2., however, there is evidence relating to the claim.

When writing, make sure that your premises are relevant to your claims. If they are not, expect *'irrelevant'* or *'so what?'* in your feedback. But relevance is only the start: now we need to assess which premises are necessary to the argument.

Necessary premises

Look at this example:

> **❝** *I bought a lottery ticket. I'm going to win a fortune.* **❞**

The premise is relevant; having a lottery ticket puts you in with a chance of winning. Since you can't the win the lottery without a ticket, it's also **necessary**. Necessary but not enough: to secure that fortune you need all six numbers. Add the second necessary premise:

43

> **"** *I bought a lottery ticket and got all six numbers. I'm going to win a fortune.* **"**

The claim now works. A necessary premise doesn't **prove** the claim but without it, the claim can't work. If a claim **needs**, but does not **have**, certain premises, then it collapses. Necessary premises are common in science and medicine. Look at this example:

> **"** *John has headaches, chills and abdominal pains.* **"**

With such general symptoms, John could have any number of illnesses:

> **"** *He lives in an area with very high incidences of malaria and was bitten last week by a mosquito.* **"**

This narrows it down. You can only catch malaria if you are bitten by a mosquito. However, this premise, though strong, still isn't enough to clinch the deal (it is only **adequate**): it is possible that John was bitten by a non-infected mosquito. Look at the final premise:

> **"** *His blood sample shows evidence of plasmodium falciparum, one of four parasites responsible for causing malignant malaria.* **"**

This settles it. If his blood contains *plasmodium falciparum,* he's got malaria. In fact, with this premise, the others are unnecessary and work simply as background information. This third premise is both **necessary** and **adequate** to prove the claim: John has malaria.

Certain claims you make will necessitate certain premises. If you can't find evidence for the premise, don't make the claim. Unsupported claims do not gain marks.

Adequate premises

Remember that for arguments to be strong, the premises need to lead to only one possibility: the claim. The lottery example needed two premises before it was adequate: the ticket plus six numbers. John's malaria, however, only needed one: the blood sample. The mosquito bite was necessary but it was not **adequate** to make the claim.

In dealing with contested knowledge, adequacy may be a matter of degree. Premises might not **prove** the claim but they **can** make it highly likely for the claim to be accepted.

Look again at the Facebook example. Bear in mind that human intelligence is an area of contested knowledge so such a claim **can never** be definitively proven. Our premises, therefore, need to make the claim **reasonable to believe**. Is the premise here adequate to support the claim?

> ❝ *Using Facebook extensively can diminish a person's intellectual ability. Sachs' (2008) study of 40 students found their IQ diminished when using Facebook for more than an hour a day.* ❞

The study provides evidence. But is one study involving only 40 individuals adequate for a strong claim like this? We need more.

> ❝ *Greenfield, a leading neuroscientist, has also expressed concern that repeated use of social networking sites*

> *shortens a user's concentration span. (Greenfield, 2010).* **"**

We've brought in a known neurologist who is well worth including. But this is expert opinion; not proof. The two premises (working separately) are still not really adequate to meet the claim. Let's add a third:

> **"** *A longitudinal study of freshmen in Boson, USA found 82% of drop-outs used Facebook for more than two hours a day (Hoffs, 2009).* **"**

The evidence is beginning to stack up. However, the claim remains unproven. If, from our wide reading, we are convinced of this link, the best course of action is to modify our claim:

> **"** *From the limited amount of research as yet undertaken, it does seem that using Facebook extensively can, in some cases, diminish a person's intellectual ability.* **"**

Our modified claim accepts the limitations of the research. From the premises given, it works. The argument is now strong.

Pitfalls to guard against

When a writer puts persuasion above precision, weak arguments often follow. Be on guard for these in your own writing and look out for them if asked to use newspaper or magazine articles.

Circular arguments

> " *University education should be free because free education is a human right.* "

The premise and the claim are the same so the argument hasn't moved forward. The writer needs to explain **why** they view free education as a human right; for example, they may argue that access to knowledge should be open to all regardless of wealth.

Inconsistency

> " *Banks were greedy and looking for profit. They put money-making second to customer service.* "

The sentences contradict each other. This can slip past if reading quickly and sometimes happen unintentionally when writing. This is why it's essential to check arguments carefully.

Black and white

> " *There's no point in giving aid to countries suffering from famine. We never give enough and they'll be in the same situation next year and the year after.* "

Here we have two extreme options. As a reader, if you can present a third option, of whatever shade of grey, you've shown the argument doesn't work.

Straw man

" *How can you justify the legalisation of drugs when it would mean millions of young people becoming addicts?* "

Here, the writer sets up an exaggerated (false) situation he will then oppose – he builds a straw man ready to burn! His argument suggests that those who agree with the legalisation of drugs must then believe his imagined consequence. With such a huge inference; the argument cannot hold.

These pitfalls are caused by faulty lines of reasoning. We started the chapter by saying that in a strong argument:

1. each premise in the line of reasoning is judged as accurate
2. the claim drawn follows logically from the premises.

We've looked at 2. It's time to judge the accuracy of the statements made. The next chapter examines how to do this.

Tips for top scores

- Take time to read arguments carefully. If you don't fully understand them it shows in your responses.

- When you spot a faulty premise, draw attention to it:
  'O'Donoghue states . . . However, it does not follow that . . .'
  This is an effective way to counter arguments in both writing and in seminar contributions.

✓ Dos	✗ Don'ts
✓ Look for the claim first when reading an argument: miss the claim and you've missed the point.	✗ Expect one rigid pattern to the line of reasoning when reading an argument.
✓ When reading, question each premise. How does it lead to the claim? Is it necessary? Adequate?	✗ Similarly, in your own writing, don't use the same line of reasoning every time. Try out different orders. Which leads to a better argument?
✓ Go through your own arguments with a fine tooth comb. Are the premises adequate? Do they lead clearly to claims?	✗ Simply state that an argument is 'a slippery slope' or a 'straw man'. State explicitly where the weakness lies.

49

5 Zooming in: reading between the lines

Academic writing should be precise, reasoned and free of unfounded assumptions. If you're new to academic writing, however, you may be unaware of your leaps in argument or the loaded terms you are using. A further problem occurs in both published texts and student work when language is ambiguous. If the reader has to make **inferences** (assumptions), it means what the writer intended and what the reader understands may differ. In written assessments, this is potentially disastrous.

Eagle-eyed scrutiny is essential to locate these problems, helping with:

- good depth of analysis
- good evaluation of source material.

To scrutinise well, we need to zoom into paragraphs, sentences and even single words to read between the lines. Research data needs to be examined just as carefully. Meticulous examination of both the arguments we read and those we write leads to a higher quality of understanding, deeper analysis and more effective evaluation – bring on that distinction!

Jumping to conclusions

Zooming in involves noticing not only the words in front of us but what is **not** there.

Missing premises

Look at the following argument:

> ❝ *More than 25% of students gained at least one A or A* at A level in 2010 compared to less than 10% in 1985* **(Premise)**. *Undoubtedly, it is far easier these days to achieve top grades* **(Claim)**. ❞

Is this the only reasonable claim to follow logically from the premise? No, there are many possible alternative claims. Perhaps the standard of teaching has improved? Or students are working harder? What is missing is a necessary premise; **evidence** of exams becoming easier. Without this, the writer has jumped to a conclusion.

Missing premises invite tutor comments such as 'not enough evidence'. When writing an argument, scrutinise each of your premises to ensure that together, they lead convincingly to the claim.

Overstating cause and effect

What is the difference between the following sentences?

1. *As the temperature increased, the ice melted.*
2. *The temperature increased. As a result, the ice melted.*

In both, there is a link between the two statements: that the first causes the second. In 2. this link is stated with signal language: *as a result*. In 1., however, the link is not stated; the reader is expected to infer.

When a link is common knowledge, as in 1., or part of the uncontested knowledge specific to your subject, this inference is fine. Not with contested knowledge, however. Look at this sentence:

3. *As women have entered the workforce, the divorce rate has shot up.*

Putting the two statements together suggests that the former **caused** the latter. But did it? The cause of both could be something else entirely – changes in the law, for instance. Avoid making inferences like this. If making a link be explicit and support your claims with evidence; otherwise you have made an unfounded assumption.

QUICK TIP

If you can see a possible but not certain relationship, you can talk about a 'correlation between variables'. This is a common phrase in research papers, meaning there is a pattern which **suggests** a link, but not enough evidence to assert anything more.

The problem with both 'missing premises' and 'overstating cause and effect' is the need to infer; **assuming** a claim from a flimsy premise or **assuming** a relationship between two factors. These habits of thinking simplify complex ideas and accept assumptions without question. Tutors have faultless antennae when it comes to unfounded assumptions. Root them out of your thinking before they do!

Rooting out assumptions

Assumptions are extremely common in everyday conversation:

Enjoy the sunshine! = *assumption that sunny days are enjoyable*

Go on, have a chocolate! = *assumption that you like chocolate.*

These work well enough in conversation, even if some people do **not** like the sun or chocolate. Academic writing, however, demands precision. Read the sentence below carefully. How many assumptions can you find?

> " *A developing country like Mexico needs investment from foreign companies in order to increase the standard of living in the population.* "

To check comprehension, restate the claim:

> " *The only way to increase the standard of living in Mexico, which is a developing country, is through investment by foreign companies.* "

Assumptions:

1. Mexico is a developing country

2. Mexico needs investment

3. This investment should come from foreign countries

4. This investment should be from companies not governments or any other sources

5. This investment would improve the standard of living

6. Mexicans want their standard of living improved.

You may be able to find more.

As with premises, each assumption, once unpacked, needs to be verified.

Let's take the first:

Mexico is a developing country.

Is it? Can the writer point to an official categorisation?

A developing country like Mexico (WTO, 2008) . . .

As long as the reference is accurate, this can now stand. If you spot an assumption in a key argument, pull it out and question it. If it does not hold, you have found a weakness and can use it to counter the argument. For example, you may find evidence that investment from foreign companies does not affect the average person's standard of living as much as investment from domestic companies. You are questioning the writer's assumption.

Assumptions are commonplace, not only in statements; zoom in closer and you can spot them within single words.

There will be a certain amount of common ground in your discipline which can be assumed: a literature student knows what a sonnet is; a physics student understands that light travels as waves. The more you know your subject, the more you'll know what can be assumed ('uncontested') and what can not. Bear in mind that a first year student may be expected to define certain terms which a third year can take as assumed knowledge. Nevertheless, whatever **is** disputed needs to be defined and unpacked.

Discriminating definitions

Some words are **not** easy to define. Try these:

- poverty
- intelligence
- masculinity.

Compare yours with the dictionary definitions. How similar were they?

Words like these are relative and can mean different things to different writers. Terms such as 'intelligence' may be contested even within a discipline – are you talking about abstract thought? Problem-solving? Emotional intelligence? Such words, therefore, need an explicit definition.

A good definition dispenses with ambiguity and tells the reader exactly where the writer is arguing from:

Masculinity in this sense can be defined as . . .

If a writer has defined a term unusually, be on guard, especially if they seem to have shaped the word to suit their argument. If the text is central to your argument, mention that the writer has used a singular definition. If it is background reading, treat the definition as contested.

> Keep your own definitions in line with common usage in your discipline. If you have read several competing interpretations of a term, you'll need to think carefully about which you accept and why. In your writing, state the definition you are using and support it with an academic source:
>
> *In line with Kyle (2005), masculinity is taken to mean . . .*

Loaded language and loose language

Loaded language

What's the difference between a freedom fighter and a terrorist? Between innocence and naivety? These words are loaded; they contain a judgement signifying the speaker's attitude. Such language appeals to emotions rather than reason – a no-no in academic writing.

Look at the following two sentences.

1. *The film was terrible.*

2. *The film has a number of faults.*

In the second sentence there is no judgement (although the reader can **infer** that the film probably isn't much good). In your own writing, unless you are using direct quotations, stick to neutral terms.

Loose language

You should be conscious by now that precision in academic language is crucial. If the meaning of a sentence is unclear or imprecise, it can be challenged.

Spot the problems with the following sentences.

1. *A mixed economy is better than a market economy.*
2. *Governments are in the pockets of big business.*
3. *A country can either be pro-Western or anti-Western.*
4. *Roman's results (2010) demonstrated that sheep can remember the faces of other sheep for up to 50 years. This proves that sheep are sentient.*

Let's see just how closely you have zoomed in. Compare your answers with the comments below.

1. Better in what way? For whom? **Better**, like **easy** or **terrible**, is a relative term which needs to be made explicit. And supported with evidence.
2. The writer's intended meaning is probably 'generally speaking' but the actual meaning is 'all governments'. By pointing out **one** exception, therefore, the argument is defeated. Be precise in usage like this; use qualifiers such as **many, the vast majority** or **some**.
3. This writer's broad strokes oversimplify. A country may be anti-Western in some aspects and pro-Western in others. It may have neither pro- nor anti-Western policies. To keep the idea but stay precise, modify the sentence: *Many countries can be broadly classified as pro-Western or anti-Western.*

4. To claim something is proven means the conclusion is beyond doubt. The results of one study cannot warrant such a strong claim; the hypothesis would need to be tested vigorously in many different types of experiment. Besides, can what happens in the mind ever be *'proven'*? Again, to be accurate the claim needs to be modified: *This **indicates** sheep **could** be sentient.*

Making accurate claims

In academic papers, accuracy is crucial to credibility.

Look again at the original and the improved claim of 4. from the last section.

This proves sheep are sentient.

This indicates sheep could be sentient.

Dramatic claims in academic papers are exceedingly rare; a narrow conclusion is the norm. In order to keep a claim accurate, writers use **hedging language**. This shows caution and allows for exceptions.

Some examples of hedging language

This evidence *suggests / indicates*	not *this shows*
This evidence *seems / appears* to demonstrate	not *this demonstrates*
This *might/ may / could / is likely to* be due to	not *this is due to*
It would seem that/ it could be argued that	not *it is*

Look for hedging language in the texts you read. Academic writers will not claim with certainty until they are **convinced** of the truth – something which, as we know, is extremely unlikely in areas of contested knowledge.

So far this chapter has focused on written arguments. However, zooming in also involves scrutinising research. While the average student takes research results as fact, the critical thinker assesses this data carefully.

Research data scrutiny

Claims from research data and statistics often seem very convincing. When used appropriately, they add credence to an argument. However, statistics, it has been said, can be used to prove anything. While scientific reports tend to be painstakingly exact in their claims, beware of writers using research data in vague terms.

Questions to ask about research data/statistics

- What claim is being made from the data?
- How exact is this claim? Examine the statistics. Words like 'majority' need further examination: was the majority 51% or 99%?
- Check the 'methods' section of any research paper or report to see what sampling method was used. Does it seem representative?
- Check in the research report how variables (factors which might affect the outcome) were controlled.
- Check the date. Are the results still relevant or have they been superseded by subsequent research?

59

- Where was the data published? Is this a trusted source?
- Who funded the research? Check that there are no vested interests, like the fish-oil company funding the study on the benefits of fish-oil.
- How big is the sample size? Bigger is better since it is easier to generalise from. A small sample is less statistically significant.
- Is this study a first? If building on previous studies, how do the results compare?

QUICK TIP

Different disciplines use and value different research methods. Follow the methods of your discipline in using and assessing this type of data. There is a wealth of books available on discipline-specific research methods.

We've zoomed in to examine assumptions and bias in language and the potential limitations of research data. Time now to zoom out. By comparing different texts, we'll gain a more complete picture of the issue under question.

Tips for top scores

- To guard against missing premises, think of your argument in terms of basic arithmetic: does Premise + Premise = Claim? If not, add another premise or modify your claim.

- Recognising and rooting out your own assumptions is difficult but is integral to a truly critical approach. Treat it like a challenge. Question everything you write. Can you back it up? Is there sufficient evidence?

■ All arguments are based on some kind of assumption and unpacking every last word becomes tedious for the reader who wants an argument to move forward. Be clear on what does **not** need to be defined as well as what does.

✓ Dos	✗ Don'ts
✓ State all premises and check for any assumptions or jumps in reasoning.	✗ Use vague or value-laden language. Make your meanings unambiguous and neutral. Write, think and rewrite until your words represent precisely what you mean.
✓ Write definitions carefully. Check in the glossaries of the books you are using to get an idea of the discipline-specific usage.	✗ Argue from different definitions of the same word. If you jump from definition to definition, logic will be lost because the terms are unstable.
✓ Look at the conclusions of academic papers and notice the use of hedging language. Use the same language in your own claims and essay conclusions.	✗ Deliberately try to mislead with statistics. Make your claims in line with your evidence even if that means modifying them.

6 Zooming out: putting texts into context

No text is written in a vacuum. Writers are human and influenced by the world around them. To assess a text, you need to zoom out and assess it in relation to others. Seeing links between writers, grouping ideas together and selecting the most appropriate texts for your purpose is synthesis, step 5 in the levels of critical thinking. This relates to two of the assessment criteria:

- identify key debates
- extensive range of sources, applied with insight.

By setting a text in its context, we see the bigger picture: how far the author's arguments tally with or challenge others in their field and how they have used and built upon arguments from earlier texts. To do this, we need to consider the author, their ideology, their intended audience and the publication in which they write.

Authors with authority

When comparing arguments, not all texts are equal. Some writers are more influential than others. A writer may be known in the field either as:

- **A key name.** *Their work may have made an important contribution to ways of thinking in your subject.*
- **An authority.** *Perhaps they have written well-regarded overviews of the field.*

A writer can be both – conducting original research as a key name and writing more general books to clarify the wider debate. As specialists in the field, their expert opinion can help strengthen your case. However, opinion, even expert, can be contested. You need to read **all** writers critically; don't take ideas as fact, no matter how famous or well-regarded the writer.

When assessing a writer's work, consider the following.

- The context in which it was written – e.g. published during the Cold War? Before Lehman Brothers went bankrupt?
- The author's prior writings: are they building on previous ideas? Have they changed perspective? Are their older publications still relevant? If so, why?
- How other writers use them: is this author widely cited? Are their ideas central to the issue? How?
- Ideology or school of thought: does the writer come from any particular position?

This last point is crucial. Rather than seeing each text as an individual piece, we need to see how it fits in with the major schools of thought of our discipline. Differing ideologies are at the heart of contested argument. Getting to grips with these will help you group texts and compare ideas comprehensively, gaining the full picture of the issue under question.

Schools of thought

A school of thought is a set of ideas based around a few key thinkers or approaches. Each shares basic assumptions as to which theories and hypotheses best explain reality.

Let's look at three major schools of thought in economics. Each has their own theory about which economic system works best.

- **Keynesian**: follows the belief that governments must regulate markets to ensure a stable economic system in the best interests of a country
- **Austrian School**: follows the belief that markets should be unregulated by governments and allowed to develop freely
- **Marxist**: follows the belief that a capitalist system is exploitative and only in the interests of an elite.

While the first two argue over whether markets should or should not be regulated by governments, the third rejects the entire notion that a market-based economy is in the interests of society. Each school, therefore, has very different beliefs which will lead to very different answers to economic questions. They may also differ in the questions they seek to explore and in their research methods. Make sure you know if an author is writing from a particular school of thought and what the basic assumptions are behind this perspective.

The intended audience

A book written for undergraduates is likely to have a different style from one written for a general audience. Stephen Hawking's books, for example, are intended for a mass audience so are less technical than his journal papers, which are written for peers, fellow professors and academics. These journal papers are likely to be the most challenging in terms of the amount of assumed knowledge between reader and writer and the depth of argument and analysis.

Your **own** writing, whether first year or postgraduate, is officially for the tutor who marks it; an expert in their field. However, you need to show you understand key concepts which your tutor clearly already knows. It may be more helpful to imagine your reader as a classmate – someone studying the same subject as you but not your particular module. That way, you'll have a clearer picture of what may need to be argued or explained.

Evaluating the publication

Just as some authors are more influential than others, some publications hold more credibility than others. If Greenfield, our neurologist from Chapter 4, writes a paper in *The British Journal of Psychiatry*, the arguments are academically useful to you. Arguments she gives in an interview with the *Daily Mail*, however, are not.

When developing your **own** argument, you need to use reputable academic knowledge **only**. If you want to go **beyond** the reading list, you will have to select sources for yourself. To do this, you need to know which type of publication is most useful. Let's evaluate some typical publications.

Textbooks, introductions and overviews

These are written to aid understanding and give you a grounding in your discipline. They often present arguments with their strengths and weakness and tell the reader which are the key debates. Be aware that some textbooks are written by an author who comes from a particular school of thought. While they will doubtless present all sides of the subject, weight given to different sections may suggest their biases. Be aware of these when using the information.

Seminal works

Certain books and papers have had a strong effect on the thinking and direction of the research within a discipline. Going back to Economics, *The General Theory* by Keynes is a highly influential piece. *Free to Choose* by Friedman is another seminal work which disputes Keynes's claims. *Das Kapital*, by Marx, is a further influential text, this time built on entirely different principles.

You will always gain a better understanding by reading the actual seminal piece rather than interpretations. After reading the original, you can see its influence in other writers and notice how the ideas have been interpreted, applied, refined and perhaps superseded. If reading an interpretation, rather than the original, don't take it as gospel. Try and read several as different writers may come to different conclusions about the significance of the text.

Journal articles

Each article in a journal is read and checked by fellow academics who pay close attention to lines of reasoning and resulting claims. Journal articles are therefore highly trusted academically. However, there are thousands of journals. Generally speaking, the more well-known a journal is, the more influential the article is likely to be. When selecting a journal article, ask the following.

■ Has your tutor or other academics recommended articles from this journal before? (If the journal is obscure, the quality may not be as high).

■ Is this journal specifically related to your discipline?

■ Do you know the writer's name? Do you recognise any of the sources in the bibliography? If not, skim the abstract to see how central it is to your research.

■ Are the references clear if you want to check the facts?

■ When was the article published? Is it still relevant?

Newspapers and weekly magazines

While it is fairly obvious that *Heat* and the *Daily Mirror* are not reputable academic sources, you may be surprised that neither are publications such as the *Independent* or *The Economist*. Articles in these publications have been checked by an editor, but have not gone through the rigorous checks of journals or academic texts. Only use these when directed by your tutor and keep your critical faculties highly attuned.

Web sources

The web is a democratic community. Academic papers are only a click away from crackpot theorists and agenda-ridden pieces. If your tutor gives a website as a source, use it. If you've found a paper yourself, evaluate it before you use it.

■ What is the URL? If the address ends with *.ac.uk*, it is from a UK academic institution. If it ends with .edu, it is from an American academic institution. These should be reputable.

■ Who produced the site? A company? An individual? For what purpose? Look at the 'about us' section for this information.

■ Is the site maintained? When was it last updated?

■ Avoid blogs. They are not peer-reviewed so have no academic authority, even if written by authors highly respected in your field. Stick to journal articles when building arguments.

Wikipedia

This is such a bugbear for tutors it deserves a section of its own. Wikipedia is **not** an academic source. It is not peer-reviewed and is open to anonymous editing which means the quality cannot be guaranteed. As a starting point to a field or theory, read it by all means. But do not use it as part of your academic argument, and never list it in your bibliography!

Primary and secondary sources

You need to be clear which type of text you are dealing with. Primary sources are authentic data; for instance, research reports in sciences and social sciences; contemporary accounts of events such as diaries and speeches in humanities or novels and paintings in the arts. Secondary sources interpret, analyse and draw conclusions from primary sources. They include textbooks, journal articles and book-length arguments.

Much of what you read is likely to be a secondary source; **interpretations** of primary research and therefore contested knowledge. Certain disciplines, such as sciences, history and law use primary sources extensively. Don't forget to evaluate primary sources just as critically as secondary sources for accuracy and credibility.

Zooming out questions

Once you've read a text, you need to situate the argument into the bigger picture. Ask yourself the following questions to help you zoom out and assess the wider context.

■ How does this text relate to other readings? Does it echo other arguments? Provide a new perspective? Contradict previous readings? Build on seminal ideas/texts?
■ How is it different? What makes it unique?
■ Do you know any texts which contradict this argument? Where does the disagreement lie?
■ Does it strengthen or weaken something else you've read? How?
■ How is it relevant for your current purpose? Where and how would you use it in your writing?

Tips for top scores

■ Make sure you know what the most influential schools of thought are in your discipline. Look at the values and assumptions behind each. If you lean towards arguments in one particular school of thought, make sure you can state explicitly why this is.

■ Make links between the texts you read. Which ones are from the same school of thought? Which argue from similar principles? Which writers' ideas do the texts build on?

■ If you doubt a writer's interpretation of a primary source (e.g. statistics), look at the reference and read it for yourself.

✓ Dos	✗ Don'ts
✓ Check each writer is referring to the same specifics when comparing arguments. For example, two texts might consider injury in athletic track events but one focuses on sprints and the other on long-distance running.	✗ Read a text out of context. If you know the author's background, their school of thought and the publication it comes from, you'll find it easier to follow.
✓ Categorise each text you read according to the writer's perspective.	✗ Reject an entire school of thought as 'wrong'. Instead, point out any assumptions they make which you find problematic. This will give you an effective critical stance.
✓ Look out for an author's ideological position; they usually state this clearly in the introduction to their text.	✗ Go too far off-piste if selecting your own sources. There are billions of books and articles out there. Always assess the writer, publication and relevance to your purpose before you devote valuable reading time to it.

PART 3

Applying critical thinking

With the tools of critical thinking firmly under your belt, it's time to apply them to your studies. Chapter 7 gives practical advice on critical reading while Chapter 8 looks at writing; how to turn those critical thoughts into A-grade assignments. The final chapter situates your thinking back into your discipline. This chapter explores how different faculties emphasise different aspects of critical thinking.

7 Reading critically

Reading is the focal point of your study. You read to prepare for seminars and lectures as well as for writing assignments. Your own academic arguments do not come from within; they come from active reading. However, the more you read, the more complex arguments become, the less black and white things seem and the more clouded an issue can get.

Reading critically takes practice. As the previous chapters have shown, critical reading involves zooming in to assess arguments and language and zooming out to take in the bigger picture. This chapter focuses on staying active and engaged with your reading as well as reading effectively. So what are you waiting for? Read on!

Reading the reading list

Critical reading skills start with deciding **what** to read. With so many new books published every year and such vast amounts of information on the internet, the ability to sort through, select and assess texts is crucial. Luckily, for most courses there is a reading list which gives a clear indication of which texts are central.

Reading lists differ. Some are long, some are short. Some are divided into key readings (often denoted with an asterisk) and further readings. Unless your reading list is very short, you aren't expected to read every text. Selection is key. Deciding what to read and how much depth to go into will depend on how much time you have and the purpose of your reading (see the 'how to read' section on the opposite page for more on this).

To decide what to read, here are some suggestions.

- Start with the key reading. Obvious, but needs to be said. 'Further reading' is extra suggestions.
- If you find key readings too difficult, look at the list to see if there's a suggested introduction to the topic. Read this first. Once you've got an overview, the more challenging readings should make more sense.
- If the reading list is short, be alert. You'll be expected to show a detailed understanding. Make sure you have got to grips with the main arguments.
- Go for the latest edition of any book unless your tutor specifically directs otherwise.
- Is it seminal? If a lot of theories and papers can be traced back to the text, read it and again. You'll probably need to come back to it again.

No reading list?

Knowing which sources to use becomes more problematic as you approach your dissertation or have to find sources for yourself. If you need to select your own sources, start with advice from your tutor. When browsing further texts, ask yourself the following.

- Have I heard this writer's name? If not, do they seem credible (publication, experience in the field, academic position)?
- From the title, does this text seem directly relevant for my purposes?
- Read the abstract/introductory paragraph. What's the aim of the text? Is it relevant?

- Does the author cite writers I know?
- Is the text saying something new for me?
- When was it written? If it mentions research, when was this carried out? Has there been later research which supports or challenges what is written here?

If the writer is unfamiliar and the above seems inconclusive, make a note of the publication for possible future use and move on; don't waste time on peripheral texts.

So you've checked your reading list and chosen the initial texts you'd like to tackle. The next question is: how should you read?

How to read

The secret to active, critical reading is purpose: know what you are looking for and bear in mind what you have read before. Much of what you read will be to write an assignment. This means forming an argument of your own in order to answer a question. Before you buckle down to read consider the following.

- What do you need to know? Keep the question you are answering or the title of the module you are preparing for firmly in mind. What is key in each text will depend on the question; this is your purpose.
- Skim the text first. If it's a book, look at the contents, index and introduction. If it's a paper, scan the abstract and introduction.
- Can you find the author's position? Knowing it helps you to predict the content and gives you a better idea of the underlying assumptions of the claims.
- Look at the final chapter or conclusion of the paper. This will provide a summary and outline the process which led to the conclusions.

■ When you find potentially useful chapters or sections, scan the first few and last few paragraphs. These give further clues as to how central the text is for your purpose and help orientate you in what the writer is going to say.

So you've found a central text – this could be a book, a paper, a chapter or a section. It's time to read.

Ways of reading

Critical reading is active, not passive; your brain is thinking, sifting, categorising, comparing and, most importantly, questioning. But even within a text, some parts may be relevant, others not. Reading everything word for word at the same speed is unstimulating and ineffective. Skimming, or even skipping, saves time which can be spent on close reading and careful assessment of central arguments. So, vary your reading speed.

> **QUICK TIP**
>
> For dissertations, you'll need to do a lot of general reading before you can get a firm idea of what will be your key texts. Keep brief notes on everything you read so that you can come back to it if necessary.

■ **Skim**: to find out if the text is worth reading; to see how the text is divided and how detailed the argument is. Skim over parts which are similar to those you've already read – especially when this is background information.
■ **Scan**: when looking for particular information. You might want to see how the writer defines a term or their take on a particular question. Use the index to find the key word then scan the relevant page to look for it.
■ **Detailed reading**: slow down when you have found something central and read more than once if necessary to fully understand the argument.

Quick reading can mean skipping key points, jumping to conclusions and only half understanding. With central arguments of central texts, you need to read carefully. This is when attention often wanders. To stay active and critical when reading closely, you need to question the text.

Questioning the text: reading as conversation

If someone is in front of you, telling you their view on an issue, you can ask questions in order to clarify, challenge and further your understanding. With a text, the writer may not be **physically** beside you but they are there on the paper, in their words.

The author writes to communicate their ideas to their readers. Think of it as a one-sided conversation. You, as the reader, provide the missing half. Enter into a dialogue with the text, just as you would in a face-to-face conversation: comment, clarify and assess. Asking the text questions keeps you active and critical. You will find many of the answers as you read; the ones you don't will keep you thinking as you read other texts or attend lectures and seminars.

Questions to ask when reading

- What do I already know about this topic?
- What do I **expect** to read?
- Is the writer coming from a particular school of thought/ stance?
- Which writers are central to this author's argument? Have I read these works?

- What's the main argument or finding? What is the writer trying to persuade me of?
- What are the premises? Are they based on facts, theories or earlier authors? Do they build a strong argument? Can I spot any flaws or inconsistencies?
- Am I convinced? Why? Why not? Can I put this in words?
- If I could ask this author one question, what would it be?

The more you read actively, the more questions like these become second nature. Active reading keeps you engaged. If you do find your mind drifting, take a break. When you return, see if you can answer any of the questions above. If not, revisit the introduction. Look at the conclusion. Try reading the first or last sentence of each paragraph to get the gist of the piece before reading again in more detail.

Dealing with counterarguments

Your reading is not complete until you have taken into account all the major perspectives on the issue. Remember that the purpose of argument is to gain a deeper understanding of the issue: pulling apart a counterargument and listing reasons why it's wrong is not in the interests of exploration of a topic. Assess the counterarguments as you would all others. In addition to the questions above, ask the following.

- Where exactly are the weaknesses? Do they dismiss or weaken the overall claim?
- Are there parts of the counterargument I think are strong? If so, will I need to modify my claims?
- Does it give solid evidence against my position? If yes, then again, how will I modify my position and narrow my claim?

■ Where the counter-argument is strong and contradicts my own strong argument, what are at the assumptions underlying each. Are we viewing the issue from different perspectives?

Note taking

Note taking is essential for remembering the main points. However, extensive note taking is time-consuming and not always helpful. Here's one way of making effective notes.

■ Write the title, author and page number at the top of a blank sheet of paper.
■ Fold this paper vertically so that it has two columns: Zoom in and Zoom out.
■ Zoom in is for the author's arguments; the answers to the 'questions to ask when reading'.
■ Zoom out is for notes which compare it to previous readings and to what you already know.

This keeps your notes succinct and relevant to your purpose.

Keeping your own stance

Another problem with endless note taking is the feeling that your own stance is fading; you forget what you originally thought as your mind fills with competing ideas. Don't worry. There's a good note taking technique for this.

Before reading, study your question and decide where you stand on it. If it's a statement, how far do you agree or disagree? Write down a percentage: 60% agree? 85% disagree? Call this your 'pre-reading' stance. Each time you read a text, go back to your percentage. Has what you've read changed your mind? What's your new stance? Write this down along with the reasons in a sentence or two. Keep going with every text you read. When it comes to writing, you will be able to see how your stance fluctuated as well as which texts were more central in building your argument. This technique takes minutes and helps you to keep your voice, the original part of your work, intact.

Tips for top scores

■ Always prioritise key texts. Plan what you will read so that you have time to gain a full understanding.

■ If reading for an assignment, start planning your answer as soon as you've read a few texts. Your plan is bound to change as you keep reading but early planning helps if you are the type to over-read, giving you more time to spend on the actual writing.

■ Read counterarguments carefully and with an open mind. Make sure you do not misrepresent counterarguments or ignore key evidence to fit your viewpoint. Academics want truth, not distortions of reality.

✓ Dos	✗ Don'ts
✓ Read to help form new opinions and arguments rather than as confirmation of what you already think.	✗ Use a text if you don't understand it. What you write is unlikely to be clear.
✓ Read key parts properly – misunderstanding an author and misrepresenting their ideas is sloppy and skews further thought.	✗ Don't necessarily read your reading list in the order given – this is very often alphabetical!
✓ Check you've got the latest edition of any published book or the edition recommended on your reading list.	✗ Get too bogged down in note taking. Get the key argument, your stance and the page number. You can always re-read if necessary.

8 Writing critically

Writing shows the breadth of your reading and the depth of your understanding. It shows your stance in relation to the various arguments and your ability to apply the knowledge you've gained to the question. If you've been thinking and reading critically, you'll already have notes and ideas ready to shape into an answer.

But let's be honest; effective academic writing isn't always easy. As an undergraduate, you are expected to argue using the key concepts, language and theories of your discipline while still learning the basics. Sounds challenging? Think of it as giving your academic opinion on a specific question using the texts you've read to support your ideas. There, that's not so bad!

Let's look again at the assessment criteria we've referred to throughout the book. This is what your tutors are looking for:

- good depth of analysis
- identifies key debates
- demonstrates an ability to think critically
- strong argument
- evidence of independent thinking
- good evaluation of source material.

By now you should have a better understanding of what these terms mean. But how do you turn critical ideas into an effective piece of writing?

Writing as conversation

When reading critically, you asked questions in order to understand the writer's argument. As a critical writer, keep the reader in mind by **anticipating** questions.

- Are you using a complicated or contested term? Define it.
- Are you giving background information? Make it clear why it's relevant.
- Are you making a claim? Support it.

Chapter 7 suggested you imagine your reader to be a student of the same discipline. Let's add to that. Imagine this student as extremely pernickety, one who delights in picking holes in arguments. You need to win them round with a sound argument and full discussion of relevant counterarguments. Let's get writing! Well no, not yet. First, you need to study your question.

Unpacking the question

Essay feedback so often begins with *'you didn't fully address the question'*. Time spent thinking and understanding what is expected of you **before** you begin writing keeps your answer relevant. This is known as unpacking the question.

Let's try this with a question related to law.

" *To what extent does the US Constitution protect interpersonal relationships?* **"**

'To what extent': this is asking for evaluation. You'll be expected to use all six critical thinking steps. *Before* planning, decide where you stand. The US Constitution fully protects interpersonal relationships (you 100% agree?); in lots of ways? (you 65% agree); hardly (you 25% agree). Your plan, and subsequent essay, depends on this.

'The US Constitution': this is straightforward. You'll need to have a copy to hand to ensure you refer to it accurately.

'Protect': define this; legal usage may be different from general usage. Also, the term in American law may be used differently from in English law.

> **QUICK TIP**
>
> Always check if your tutor has a preferred version of core text: for example, the Oxford edition of *Pride and Prejudice* rather than the Penguin edition.

'Interpersonal relationships': this is quite a loose phrase. It could mean romantic relationships, families or even business associations. Your definition influences how the argument moves forward. You may need to narrow the definition to a few pertinent features in order to deal with issues in sufficient depth.

Once you have unpacked the questions and decided on your stance, you can begin to plan your answer.

Planning your answer

Your plan is your thinking on paper. A disorganised essay is hard to follow. Jumping illogically from one idea to the next is the hallmark of an essay without a plan. The plan keeps you on track and prevents you from getting lost in irrelevant material or long-winded explanations. It is a place to experiment and move things around.

Ideally, start planning while you are still reading. Note down links, contradictions and, of course, strong arguments. For the actual essay plan, write the question in the centre of a blank A4 page and ask the following.

- What is my overall argument in relation to the question? Write this underneath the question.
- What are my reasons? These will become my subsidiary arguments. As a rule of thumb, go for one paragraph per argument. Space these around the page.
- Where do ideas from the texts fit in? Write the text reference next to the relevant subsidiary argument.
- If I am using ideas from several texts to make one point, which order seems most effective? Experiment. Then mark the order on the page: 1, 2, 3.
- How do counterarguments fit? Will I concede any points from these? Write them in.
- Which points are linked? How should I group ideas together? Draw lines linking ideas together.

Bear in mind your word count while you plan. Work out how much depth you can go into **before** you write. This avoids having to cut well-constructed paragraphs because your essay is overlong.

QUICK TIP

Go through your notes and decide which parts can be used as evidence or argument. Which could be used for background description or explanation? Don't try and cram in everything you've read. Selection is paramount! Everything that **does** go in should be contributing to the overall argument.

Getting started

Do you fear the blank page? Dread the empty screen? Some of the best writers have trouble getting those first words down. Free-writing is an invaluable technique to overcome writer's block. For the only time in this book, it's imperative to avoid critical thinking!

You have five minutes. Start the clock. Write down whatever comes into your mind related to the question. No crossing out, no deciding it's useless. Whatever it is, write it down. When the time's up, turn your critical powers back on and read your free-write. Anything in there of use? Remember that you don't have to use **any** of your first ideas. They are stepping stones to your final piece.

With your pen raring to go and your plan in front of you, it's time to shape your thoughts into an assignment. For effective academic writing, you'll need to plan and shape each paragraph just as carefully as the overall piece.

Critical paragraphs

Each paragraph of the main body of your writing is a place to develop a subsidiary argument, one which contributes to the main claim. A main body paragraph needs as a minimum:

- a central claim
- premises
- evidence (statistics, examples, and support from key academic sources to back up both claims and premises)
- definitions of any disputed terms.

> **QUICK TIP**
>
> The introductory paragraph sets the question into a context and spells out your argument: *'this essay will'*. The conclusion restates the argument, recapping the reasons you arrived at your stance.

Position of the claim

The most common position of the claim is at the beginning of the paragraph:

Here's what I think **(claim)** *and here's why* **(premises)**.

Putting the claim first makes your position clear. This is the most common position for a claim so, if in doubt, follow this pattern.

Another possible position for the claim is at the end of the paragraph:

Here is some important information building to something **(premises)**. *This is what I conclude from these premises* **(claim)**.

This works well for persuasive purposes: 'read these premises', it suggests, 'and you will have no option but to come to the same conclusion'.

A less common but still possible position is the middle of a paragraph:

Here's a reason **(premise)** *which leads to my claim. Recent evidence, which I'm citing here for you, backs up this claim* **(further premise)**.

Use this if your first premise links to a point from the previous paragraph and then leads to the claim. Perhaps the further premise will link to the next paragraph.

Think about your paragraphs carefully. Where would the claim work best?

Using sources

Your references show which books and writers influenced your thinking. For your assignment to be academically valid, you **must** refer to academic sources. Use ideas from these:

- to illustrate a point you're making
- as evidence for your reasoning
- to support your claim
- as evidence that a counterargument is weak.

Think about how you will integrate sources into your writing. Use quotations sparingly, making sure it's clear **why** you have quoted; word for word citation, remember, is at step 1 of the stages of critical thinking. Certain subjects such as literature, however, may expect a larger number of direct quotations, so work within the guidelines of your discipline. *Student Essentials: Essay Writing* goes into more detail about effective use of sources.

Regaining your voice: originality

Assessment criteria for a distinction almost always mention originality. However originality doesn't mean conducting new research or crafting a never-before considered perspective. It is **your** take on the specific assignment. The way you weave ideas from your sources to answer the question effectively gives you a unique and therefore original answer. Always construct your own argument rather than parroting someone else's.

For example, imagine you are answering the law question from the previous section:

" *To what extent does the US Constitution protect interpersonal relationships?* "

The first text, by Scullion, argues that the US Constitution can be interpreted differently depending on whether it is *protection* or *freedom* of individuals which is being questioned. This is really useful. You agree with Scullion. However, Scullion is not writing specifically on interpersonal relationships. The second text, by Buxton, about homosexuality and the US Constitution, is central but only to part of your argument as it only focuses on one type of relationship. A third text, by Madgin, opposes some of Scullion's arguments but makes some interesting points which Scullion has not considered. You'll include these in your essay. Your stance is now different to Scullion's. However, Madgin's ideas are not fully supported, so you'll draw attention to this. That's it! Your original response! No-one else thinks quite like you.

Questioning your first draft

You've followed your plan and written the first draft. This is not your final answer. To assess your work effectively, try to leave it at least overnight before starting on the second draft. Use the following as a checklist.

Organisation and content

- Is my position clear?
- Is the conclusion clear?
- Does each claim have premises and text support? Is the line of reasoning easy to follow?
- Does each paragraph have a structure?
- Where is the best place for the claim?

- How does my line of reasoning work?
- Is the background description all necessary? For each sentence, ask *'Why am I saying this'*? How does it relate to the question?
- Is my language clear and without assumptions, loaded or loose language?
- Have I given counterarguments full consideration, bringing in the perspectives from all main schools of thought?

Sources

For your work to stand up as an academic piece, sources need to be used effectively. Ask yourself these questions about your sources.

- Have I related readings to the question and to my stance?
- Am I using sources to tell the reader something?
- Have I shown evaluation of the arguments rather than simply repeating them?
- Have I paraphrased text arguments without misrepresenting the ideas?
- For each reference, ask yourself *'Why have I cited this person'*?

If possible, ask a fellow student to read and comment on your work, focusing on clarity and quality of argument. Bear in mind any tutor feedback you've had from previous essays. And keep in mind the three 'c's: critical, convincing and concise.

Tips for top scores

- Keep your language formal and impersonal and double check it for typos – handing in an essay with basic mistakes is like going to a job interview with ketchup on your chin.

- Remember the aim of an argumentative essay is to persuade the reader of your stance. This may mean playing around with the order of your content to see which makes the best argument.

- Start your argument with the most important or controversial aspects. These show the reader you know what is most central to the debate.

✓ Dos	✗ Don'ts
✓ Ask your tutor if you do not understand an assignment question.	✗ Write without a clear plan; it's like driving without a map.
✓ Keep referring back to the question to check you are on track.	✗ Necessarily go for the first order that suggests itself when planning. Imagine the different paths the writing could take.
✓ Check each argument you make is directly relevant to the question and supports your conclusion.	✗ Keep the reader in suspense. State in the first paragraph what your essay will argue.
✓ For each paragraph ask yourself – what point am I making? How does it relate to the question?	✗ Try and squeeze in everything you know. You need space for the main argument.
✓ Account for any weaknesses in your argument – show what they are and how they lead to a modified conclusion.	✗ Make large claims unintentionally. Use hedging language to ensure accuracy. Help the reader by linking parts together and using signalling language.

9 Critical thinking in the disciplines

Each discipline has evolved its own approach to its own central questions. Which aspects of critical thinking are emphasised depends on the object of study and the aims of the research. This chapter takes a brief look at critical approaches in three broad subject classifications: science; arts and humanities, and social sciences. There is not always a clear-cut division between these groupings; business studies, for instance is classified as either humanities or social sciences depending on the approach favoured by the particular department of a university. Use this chapter as a starting point to get you thinking about approaches in your chosen subject.

Critical thinking in the sciences

For scientists, the object of study is the universe and the natural world: objective reality. The aim of science is to explain the universe and predict future natural events.

Methods and critical implications

Scientific study is empirical, based on careful observation and experiment. Scientific thought assumes that the same cause operating under the same conditions will result in the same effects at any time; for example, that water kept at 0 degrees will always freeze. Accepted theories, laws and principles are taken as uncontested and applied to research.

QUICK TIP

Theories may be uncontested but they are **not** facts. New theories do arise and supersede accepted thought. A critical scientist must be open to alternative possibilities.

Science deals with two types of research question: those with one verifiable answer; for instance, *why do petals have different colours?* and contested questions such as *why do humans have an appendix?* For the latter, you must evaluate the competing arguments and come to a reasoned scientific judgement. Make sure you know which type of question **you** are answeing.

Critical implications

- Careful observation and systematic study are far more important than quick thinking. Research needs to be analysed for flaws, inconsistencies and limitations.
- Results need to be tested, modified and refined before claims are made. These claims need to be exact with a meticulous line of reasoning and are usually tentatively expressed.
- The line of reasoning needs to be analysed closely for precision and logic, whether expressed in mathematical formula or academic language. Pay close attention to premises: the distinction between necessary, sufficient and contributing causes is essential in both pure and applied science.
- Writing must be clear and well-organised. Valid scientific results are verifiable (repeatable). The method, therefore, needs to be written so clearly and explicitly that a reader could copy the experiment and gain the same results.
- Questioning is central to scientific thought. Questions such as *'What if I try this?'* and *'What do my results mean?'* are used to create new hypotheses.

Critical thinking in arts and humanities

The object of study in humanities is the written text while in the arts it is the artefact. Both cultural products created by individuals. The aim in studying arts and humanities is to make sense of and better understand the human condition. There is no objective truth to uncover; interpretation is key. Questions such as *'How well did Shakespeare portray women?'* have no correct answer. As humans studying human constructs, arguments are recognised as subjective and inevitably contested.

Methods and critical implications

In interpretation, of texts or artefacts, all is contested, from the writer's or artist's intended message, to the context in which it was created, to the meaning of the words themselves. This does not mean, however, that anything goes. Interpretation is informed, critical opinion and certain key thinkers will have authority in each discipline.

Critical implications

- There is no one agreed methodological approach; multiple perspectives are commonplace. Claims are usually made and supported in the light of a particular framework of analysis, such as feminism or postmodernism. These theoretical methodologies come under the heading of critical theory and include gender studies, marxism, psychoanalysis, deconstruction and post-structuralism.
- Critical theories are not necessarily in opposition but they work on different assumptions and explore different questions. Which theories are central to your study depends not only

95

on your subject but on your university department and the interests of your tutor.

■ Critical theories challenge accepted notions of thought. Deep analysis involves unpacking the assumptions of both creator and critic.

■ Any evaluation must consider different perspectives. Which ones will depend on the question, the module you have taken and again, the interests prevalent in the university department.

Critical thinking in the social sciences

In social science, the object of study is human behaviour and society. The aim of research is to capture and understand how societies work; how people in groups interact and behave. How research is best conducted, however, is itself contested.

Methods and critical implications

In Social Sciences expert disagreement plays a major part with multiple competing perspectives on how to conduct research. Let's simplify these into two broad camps.

1. **Empirical:** Empiricists argue that using the same methods as science reveals an objective reality and provides valid replicable results. Laboratory experiments are used as well as quantitative methods such as surveys and questionnaires and results from this data are used to generalise from and form theories. Using empirical methods to understand human behaviour, however, can be tricky. There are countless variables in humans, from age, to gender, to race, to region, to educational background etc., all of which can affect results, and problems abound in replicating research.

2. Interpretative: Interpretivists believe that human experience is unique and cannot be quantified. Qualitative methods, such as extended interviews or longitudinal case studies are used to gain a deeper understanding of human experience. These methods, however, do not produce the type of data from which generalisations can be made.

Luckily, the two camps are no longer at loggerheads. Many researchers triangulate, that is, use both types of research to provide a fuller picture. For instance if studying voting patterns, results from a questionnaire give a broad overview of patterns of behaviour while extended interviews provide rich and detailed data. Nevertheless, much research is criticised on the grounds that it is too empirical or too interpretivist. When looking at an argument based on research results, methods must be carefully assessed.

Critical implications

- As a social scientist, always take a position. However, keep this position open to change.
- Key questions such as *'What is a good education*?' or *'How should prisons be run*?' feature widely in everyday media reports. However, these complex issues tend to be simplified, reduced and 'solved' when in reality there are no such clear-cut answers. Social scientists need to stay judgement-free and expect complexity when dealing with social issues.
- Whether human behaviours can be studied objectively is up for debate. For a start, humans often behave differently when placed in a laboratory situation. Other problems include unintentional researcher bias: for instance, the type of questions asked in a questionnaire can often determine the results.

- With so much material, both academic and general, it is easy to be too selective. Research may result in partial truths which can be as misleading as falsehoods. Social scientists must consider **all** key perspectives; synthesising arguments is essential.

Critical thinking in *your* discipline

It is clear that a critical approach is paramount whatever you study. Professors and lecturers are specialised in their fields and used to thinking from within their subject. You need to do the same. Consider **your** discipline:

- what are the key debates?
- how much knowledge can be taken as fact?
- what methods should I use in my studies?
- what makes a successful argument?
- what is good evidence?

Thinking within your discipline does not, however, mean ignoring the bigger picture. Average students tend to compartmentalise what they learn rather than noticing crossovers and interconnections between modules and between disciplines. The ability to show synthesis in thinking is especially important for those doing a joint honours or a combined degree.

Essays, experiments, presentations and portfolios all make different demands on students but all expect a critical approach with detailed analysis and careful thinking. The knowledge you gain from reading and lectures is your raw material. By thinking, analysing and evaluating, you transform it for your purposes. Now you're on the road to a critical approach it's time to get studying! Good luck!

Tips for top scores

- For further research on how critical thinking is approached in your subject, invest in a discipline-specific book.

- Read the description of your course in your university prospectus and compare it to other universities. What differences in emphasis and approach are there?

- When writing, if your argument is closely aligned to one particular school of thought, make this explicit. Make sure you consider other perspectives and challenges to your perspective and rebuttals to these.

✓ Dos	✗ Don'ts
✓ Pay attention to the texts you read as they show the way of thinking which is expected in your subject. For example, how are statistics used?	✗ Assume that even within the same faculty, ways of arguing and presenting knowledge will be the same.
✓ Read your handbook carefully for advice on how to approach your studies.	✗ Assume that a creative task involves only your personal thought. Your ideas need to be grounded in the academic readings and ideas within your discipline.
✓ Examine research papers critically, whoever the author; peer review does not catch all problems.	✗ Stop questioning. It will keep you critical, whatever your subject.

Critical thinking Q&A

What is critical thinking?
Critical thinking is careful, reasoned thinking, based on analysing and assessing the knowledge you encounter, rather than accepting it at face-value. See the Introduction and Chapter 2 for more information.

Why is critical thinking important at university?
Because it shows you can think for yourself. Knowledge at university is complex and there are thousands of new papers and publications every year. You need to be able both to articulate why some theories and arguments are stronger than others and to build your own academic arguments. Furthermore, critical thinking is **expected** by your tutors so, without it, grades are likely to be average or poor.

How can I be more critical?
By developing a questioning approach to your studies. Ask *'Why?'* *'How?'* *'So what?'* *'What if?'* in order to dig deep into your subject. In addition, always consider alternative answers to questions rather than accepting the first one you find. See Chapter 1 to find out more.

How do I evaluate?
Evaluate means to judge. Ask how important or useful the text you have read is. Is the argument original? Is it sound? Is it based on valid assumptions? Does it lead to new ideas and research? Evaluation involves understanding, analysing, synthesising and applying. See Chapter 2 to learn more.

How do I form a convincing argument?
Make sure you have all three essential components: claim, premises and an attempt to persuade the reader to your

viewpoint. Plan your argument carefully, making sure that it is fully supported with ideas from academic texts. Check there is a line of reasoning running through the whole piece which builds logically and persuasively to the conclusion. See Chapters 3 and 4 for more.

How can I read critically?
Form questions about the text which your reading will answer; what is the writer trying to persuade me? What reasons do they give? Look for the writer's main message (**the argument**) and the reasons they give (**the line of reasoning**). Assess these. See Chapters 4, 5 and 7 for more on this.

What's a school of thought?
This is a group of thinkers who value certain theories, work from certain assumptions, ask similar questions and share a similar approach to ideas under study. In your discipline, there may be several major schools of thought you'll need to become familiar with. Chapter 6 has more information.

How can I write critically?
Work out what the assignment is asking of you. Be aware that evaluation is central to most essay questions; don't simply repeat information but **use** it to build a persuasive argument in answer to the question set. See Chapter 8 to learn more.

How does critical thinking differ from subject to subject?
Each discipline has its own academic conventions which have evolved and developed over time. Empirical research methods (using observation and experimentation) work well when studying the natural world but if the object of study is a Greek sculpture then interpretation is needed. When human behaviour is under study (as in social sciences), both empirical and interpretative methods are used and a key debate is over which provides the best results. See Chapter 9 for more detail.

Glossary

Argument
A point of view with supporting premises which is intended to persuade others.

Analyse
Examine in close detail to discover meaning, essential features etc.

Assessment criteria
The standards on which assessed work is judged.

Assumption
A belief which is taken for granted as true.

Claim
A belief which the speaker/writer believes to be true based on premises.

Contested knowledge
Knowledge which is open to question and debate.

Counterarguments
Arguments which oppose your own.

Evaluate
To carefully judge the strengths and weaknesses of a text, using a set of standards.

Infer
To hint or imply without stating explicitly

Line of reasoning
The way premises and claims link to create a clear chain of thought.

Overall argument
The main claim of the argument, be it a page, a chapter or an entire book.

Premise
A reason which you believe to be true and which leads to a claim.

Subsidiary argument
The arguments in a text which, taken together, lead to your overall claim.

Uncontested knowledge
Knowledge that can be taken as valid and applied without the need to question it critically.